the unquenchable worshipper

matt redman

David C Cook
transforming lives together

THE UNQUENCHABLE WORSHIPPER
Published by David C Cook
Kingsway Communications LTD
Lottbridge Drove, Eastbourne BN23 6NT, England

David C Cook
4050 Lee Vance View, Colorado Springs, CO 80918 U.S.A.

David C Cook Distribution Canada
55 Woodslee Avenue, Paris, Ontario, Canada N3L 3E5

ISBN 978-1-4347-0484-9

Previously published with the ISBN 978-0-85476-995-7

Cover Design: Amy Konyndyk
Cover Image: Veer Images

Printed in the United States of America
First Edition 2001

1 2 3 4 5 6 7 8 9 10

123011

Dedicated to Beth and Maisey.

Maisey, you are an amazing gift from God to us.

I pray that you grow up to be a 'burning

worshipper' of Jesus, just like your mum.

thanks

Thank you, Beth, for loving me and spurring me on with God. Thank you, Mike, for your friendship, encouragement and generosity—you have taught me so much. Thanks also to all those I've been privileged to walk alongside and learn from on this journey of exploring worship music: Martin Smith, Les Moir, Andy Piercy, Graham Kendrick, Noel Richards, Louie Giglio, Kevin Prosch, Andy Park, Bryn Haworth. Lastly, to David and Mary P—you'll never know how much you've done.

contents

preface to the new edition

Welcome to the tenth anniversary edition of *The Unquenchable Worshipper*. It's a pleasure to be writing a fresh preface for this new version. When I first thought about the theme of *unquenchable worship,* I hadn't initially intended for it to become a book. I was planning some teaching one day and stumbled upon a little flow of words which all began with an *un* and all were inspiring worship attributes. I soon realised I had ten of these, and only then did it dawn on me that they might become chapter titles for the framework of a book. I wasn't sure I had anything earth-shatteringly new to say, but I thought maybe I'd found an interesting way to revisit some important truths. Incidentally, that's really the same thing that happens when you write a worship song. You're never creating new truth or discovering a concept no one else has ever thought of. Indeed, there's nothing new under the sun. All you are really doing is searching for a fresh and inspiring way to visit that age-old revelation. As someone once said, the best songs take universal themes and express them in unique ways.

Over the years, I've loved trying to study and explore the place that music can play in our worship. It fascinates me that throughout the journey of Scripture, the people of God so often used melody, rhythm, and lyric to help them talk to God together. The Bible itself contains a whole songbook—the Psalms—which would have been the songbook of Jesus as He walked upon this earth. But as special a part as music can play in expressing our devotions individually or gathered, it is never the *be all and end all.* If it is to mean anything, we must always complete the integrity of our offerings with lives laid down in love and service. The main message of *The Unquenchable Worshipper* is that God has always looked for more than a song. As St. Augustine once reminded us:

> Don't let your life give evidence against your tongue. Sing with your voices, sing also with your hearts; sing with your mouths, sing also with your conduct.[1]

Yes, let's use our musicality to bring praise to Jesus—for that is a powerful and meaningful way to revere Him. But ultimately may our lives themselves become the song—our words, thoughts, and deeds flowing together in beautiful harmony. As you make that your life's aim, I hope this little book propels you along the way.

Matt Redman
January 2012

1
the unquenchable worshipper

Enter, the unquenchable worshipper. This world is full of fragile loves—love that abandons, love that fades, love that divorces, love that is self-seeking. But the unquenchable worshipper is different. From a heart so amazed by God and His wonders burns a love that will not be extinguished. It survives any situation and lives through any circumstance. It will not allow itself to be quenched, for that would heap insult on the love it lives in response to.

These worshippers gather beneath the shadow of the cross, where an undying devotion took the Son of God to His death. Alive now in the power of His resurrection, they respond to such an outpouring with an unquenchable offering of their own.

The Bible is full of unquenchable worshippers—people who refused to be dampened, discouraged or distracted in their quest to glorify God. I love the heart attitude of the prophet Habakkuk, who decided he would choose to respond to God's worth, no matter how bleak a season he found himself in:

> Though the fig-tree does not bud and there are no grapes on the vines, though the olive crop fails and the fields produce no food, though there are no sheep in the pen and no cattle in the stalls, yet I will rejoice in the LORD, I will be joyful in God my Saviour. (Habakkuk 3:17–18)

In Acts 16, Paul and Silas also resolved to overcome less-than-favourable conditions and worship God. You would have forgiven them if they weren't in the mood for singing, sitting in their jail cell. They'd been unjustly arrested, beaten, 'severely' flogged, and thrown into the deepest part of the prison, with their feet in stocks. Yet, somehow, Paul and Silas found it in themselves to sing out praise to God. Refusing to let their souls be dampened, they worshipped with everything they had left.

Most of us don't own fig trees and haven't been in prison for being a Christian, but the principle is the same for us as it was for Habakkuk, Paul and Silas—we can always find a reason to praise. Situations change for better and for worse, but God's worth never changes.

I once heard the story of Fanny Crosby, the American hymn writer of the nineteenth century. She described a life-changing incident that happened to her as a baby:

> When about six weeks old I was taken sick and my eyes grew very weak and those who had charge of me poulticed my eyes. Their lack of knowledge and skill destroyed my sight forever. As I grew older

> they told me I should never see the faces of my friends, the flowers of the field, the blue of the skies, or the golden beauty of the stars.... Soon I learned what other children possessed, but I made up my mind to store away a little jewel in my heart which I called 'Content.'[1]

In fact Fanny Crosby was only eight years old when she wrote this song:

> O what a happy soul am I!
> Although I cannot see,
> I am resolved that in this world
> Contented I will be.
>
> How many blessings I enjoy,
> That other people don't.
> To weep and sigh because I'm blind,
> I cannot, and I won't.[2]

And this contented worshipper went on to write around eight thousand hymns of praise. Those thousands of songs were simply the result of a fire that burned in her heart for Jesus and could not be put out. Someone once asked her, 'Fanny, do you wish you had not been blinded?' She replied, in typical style, 'Well, the good thing about being blind is that the very first face I'll see will be the face of Jesus.'

Many might have chosen the path of bitterness and complaint as their response to God, but she chose the path of contentment and praise. The choice between these two paths faces us each day, with every situation that's thrown our way. Bitterness dampens and eventually destroys love for God. It eats away at the statement 'God is love' and tells us He is not faithful. But contentment does the opposite: it fuels the heart with endless reasons to praise God.

And there *are* endless reasons to praise Him. I once heard Pete Waterman (of production team Stock, Aitken and Waterman) talking about love songs in the world of pop music. He cynically suggested that you can write only four songs—'I love you,' 'I hate you,' 'Go away' and 'Come back.' I'm thankful, as someone who writes worship songs, that there's a lot more songwriting material to get your heart into than that! I'll never be able to think, 'Right, that's God pretty much wrapped up … what shall I write about next?' The brightness of His glory and the wonders of His heart will no doubt have us pouring out new songs for all eternity.

At the end of Song of Songs comes a fantastic declaration of unquenchable worship:

> Love is as strong as death, its jealousy unyielding as the grave. It burns like blazing fire, like a mighty flame. Many waters cannot quench love; rivers cannot wash it away. (Song of Songs 8:6–7)

Too often my worship is tamed by the complications and struggles of this world. But I long to be in a place where my fire for God cannot be quenched or washed away, even by the mightiest rivers of opposition—a worship which can never be extinguished.

Fire extinguishers work by removing one of the three things needed to keep a fire ablaze: heat, oxygen and fuel. So, in other words, there are three main ways to put a fire out: cool the burning material with water (or some other such substance), cut off the oxygen or cut off the supply of fuel.

And I think there's a parallel here with our hearts of worship. We long to be a people whose hearts burn for God, but if we're not careful, there are ways we can lose something of that fire.

First, just as water can put a fire out, so, too, the pressures and the trials of this life can dampen our hearts of worship. It's so easy in a time of hardship to 'cool off' a bit, and lose that sense of wonder and trust. We ask why God would let such things happen to us, and we wind down our worship, kidding ourselves that we'll start up again when things are better. Or maybe we don't 'feel' like worshipping anymore, so we don't. I've seen many worshippers thrown off course by difficult situations. But I've also seen people who have endured even more difficult situations and emerged with their hearts of worship burning as strongly as ever, if not stronger.

There is a kind of worshipper who 'always trusts, always hopes, always perseveres,' and who gets through the storms of life with a heart still blazing. Sometimes it comes down to a simple choice. We may be hard pressed on every side, weary and not able to sense God. But then a choice faces us—to fix our eyes on the circumstances, or to cling on to God and choose to worship Him, even when it hurts. The heart of God loves the offerings of a persevering worshipper. Though overwhelmed by many troubles, they are even more overwhelmed by the beauty of God.

The second way to extinguish a fire is to cut off the oxygen. In worship terms, this means to quench the Holy Spirit. It's plain from the Bible that we worship by the Holy Spirit (Philippians 3:3), but it's also clear that the Holy Spirit can be grieved. Ephesians 4:30 urges us: 'Do not grieve the Holy Spirit of God.' Then it tells us some of the ways not to grieve Him: 'Get rid of all bitterness, rage and anger.' The implications of this are huge. Take our church services, for example. We talk a lot about 'Spirit-led worship,' but if we truly want to be led by the Holy Spirit, we need to make sure we're keeping in step with Him in our everyday lives. As a worship leader, this is a challenging and even scary thought. I need to make sure that I'm making my life an appropriate dwelling place for Him. An unquenchable, burning worshipper needs to be full of the Holy Spirit.

The third way of stopping a fire is to cut off the fuel it thrives on. If you've ever watched TV footage of a forest fire, you may have noticed the fire fighters burn or chop away a whole section of forest so that when the fire reaches that place, it cannot spread any further.

The revelation of God is the fuel for the fire of our worship. And there is always more fuel for the fire. When we open the eyes of our hearts, God's revelation comes flying at us from so many different angles. He's revealed Himself to us in creation, throughout the history of His people, and overwhelmingly at the cross. And to this day, every breath we breathe is a reminder of our Maker, and every hour holds the possibility of living in His presence. We simply need to keep putting ourselves in a place where we're likely to receive this revelation. The heart of worship is fuelled by essential things such as reading God's Word, praying to Him and going to church to share fellowship together. There are other ways too, such as getting out into nature—the ocean, the mountains, or just a field—to soak our souls in the wonder of our Creator.

Romans 1:20 tells us there's no excuse for those who don't believe, as God has revealed who He is to everyone through all He's created.

When my wife, Beth, and I had our first child—a beautiful little daughter called Maisey—I wondered how people could ever deny the existence of God after having witnessed the birth of a baby. The nine months leading up to Maisey's birth were a fascinating time and spoke volumes to us of the wonder of God and His creation. Ultrasound scans gave a fantastic insight into her growth and development. How could it be that this tiny baby was living and kicking, her little heart beating inside the body of my wife? How could she be so well formed, with miniature fingernails, at such an early stage? I was amazed at the goodness of God to us, and with the wonder of what He had made. Every little movement and kick I felt when I placed my hand on Beth's stomach was the revelation of God to me.

So often when my worship has dried up, it's because I haven't been fuelling the fire. I haven't set aside any time to soak myself under the showers of God's revelation. Often time is the key factor. But if we can find space to soak ourselves in God's Word, His presence, His creation, and spend time with other believers, then we'll find that the revelation floods back into our lives, and our hearts will respond with a blaze of worship once more.

Earlier in this chapter I mentioned worshipping God even in our darkest hour. But that doesn't mean we're to be 'shiny, happy'

Christians, living in unreality, and not admitting when there are things wrong in our lives. There's definitely a place for brokenness and weeping in worship, but there's a right way and a wrong way to express this.

When we pour out our heart-cries to God, they mustn't ever become a criticism of who He is. Apparently, about 70 percent of the Psalms are laments—in other words, songs of sorrow and crying out.[3] A true lament never challenges or questions the worth of God. Instead, it knows that His goodness and greatness are the only hope for a bleak situation. Even at our lowest ebb there should be an underlying trust, and therefore worship. It's a precious song of praise that can overcome any obstacle and rise from the heart of the troubled believer to the very heart of God. Such songs cry out, 'Even in my darkest hour I can still glimpse the brightness of Your worth and the goodness of Your heart. I am in a desperate state, but no circumstance or trial could ever overshadow You.' It is praise that costs, even hurts. But sacrifices often hurt.

The Psalms have in fact been described as praise in the presence and absence of God.[4] In other words, a worship which survives every situation, whether God seems close or nowhere to be found. These laments are deep cries to God from a place of despair. But is that really 'worship,' or is it simply 'complaining'? In one sense, yes, they are complaints. These petitions to God are the worship songs of a broken people. But almost without exception they also display an underlying confidence and trust in God, and so are truly worship. As B. W. Anderson explained, 'The laments are really expressions of praise, offered in a minor key in the confidence that Yhwh is faithful.'[5]

I love Psalm 89 for that reason. At first glance it doesn't look like a lament at all. Starting with the optimistic lyric 'I will sing of the LORD's great love forever,' it seems to be the worship song of an untroubled heart. But that isn't the case. When we get to verse 49 we discover the struggle going on in the psalmist's soul: 'O Lord, where is your former great love, which in your faithfulness you swore to David?'

Hasn't he just contradicted himself? He seems to thank God for His great love and then wonder where it is. Exactly! At present he cannot see or feel the measure of God's love, yet he knows it to be as real and strong as it ever was. He's a man who's looked over God's track record and found it to be perfect. And so he rises up with an unquenchable song of faith and trust.

Jesus Himself used the words from the Psalms of lament as He suffered the cruelty of the cross. In agony of heart, mind, body and spirit, He cried out, 'My God, my God, why have you forsaken me?' from Psalm 22. It is a cry of torment, yet of strangely submissive devotion. The Son of God then breathes His last with a verse from Psalm 31—another lament psalm: 'Into your hands I commit my spirit' (v. 5). Amazingly, at this point of utter torment, Jesus is offering up the common worship songs of His day. And in so doing He becomes an inspiration to us. Whatever trials lie ahead in this life, unquenchable worshippers are found with a song of undying worship on their lips.

2

the undone worshipper

> In the year that King Uzziah died, I saw the Lord sitting on a throne, high and lifted up, and the train of His robe filled the temple. Above it stood seraphim.... And one cried to another and said: 'Holy, holy, holy is the LORD of hosts; the whole earth is full of His glory!' And the posts of the door were shaken by the voice of him who cried out, and the house was filled with smoke. *So I said: 'Woe is me, for I am undone!* Because I am a man of unclean lips, and I dwell in the midst of a people of unclean lips; for my eyes have seen the King, the LORD of hosts.' (Isaiah 6:1–5 NKJV)

Before the throne of God, the prophet Isaiah becomes an undone worshipper. Often when we meet with God we experience His gentleness and comfort. But this was an altogether different kind of meeting, a holy moment marked out by discomfort and soul-searching. The prophet encounters the Lord Almighty and is never the same again. He realises God's greatness and, in the light of that, his own weakness: 'Woe is me, for I am *undone*!'

Isaiah is broken, stunned and shaken in the presence of God. But this brokenness is not a destructive thing; God is stripping him apart in order to put him back together as a stronger, purer worshipper—a worshipper whose heart-cry is, 'Here am I. Send me!' (v. 8). Of course there's a time in worship to be joyful, content and even comfortable. But there also comes a time when God will make us distinctly uncomfortable. He puts us under the spotlight of His holiness, where we begin to search our hearts ever more closely. Richard Foster called it 'God's scrutiny of love.'[1] It's God's tough love—often severe, though always an act of kindness and never cruelty. He's a holy King, insisting on a holy people. Yet He's also the perfect Father, disciplining the ones He loves, simply because He loves them.

Several years ago I went to a Worship Together conference in the USA as one of the worship leaders. As usual I tried to prepare my heart and think about what God was wanting to do. But the best preparation for me came in the first session of worship, led by one of the other worship leaders.

As I stood in the congregation, God's presence invaded my heart in a new and powerful way. But it wasn't one of those tender, reassuring times. All it did was make me want to repent. Rising to the surface of my heart came those little unspoken attitudes and thoughts which had passed by unnoticed, and which I now saw had offended the heart of God. Little bits of pride, and feeding too much off other people's support, instead of looking for my heavenly Father's approval.

'Why on earth am I here as a worship leader?' I wondered. 'I need to be here just to get right with God in the congregation, off the stage.' I was an undone worshipper.

But that's exactly how God wanted it. When I got up to lead the next session, He didn't want me thinking I could achieve something, or that I had something special to give. He desired a broken and dependent heart. As King David, 'Israel's singer of songs,' discovered, 'the sacrifices of God are a broken spirit; a broken and contrite heart, O God, you will not despise' (Psalm 51:17).

The book of Jonah also gives us some clues about how God works in the hearts of undone worshippers. When it came to being a worshipper, Jonah obviously counted himself in: 'I worship the LORD, the God of heaven,' he said in chapter 1, verse 9.

But his credentials were severely tested when he was told to deliver a very harsh word to a very scary people. We all know the story—he decided that wasn't his calling, ran away, and ended up in the belly of a huge fish. Being inside a fish gives you time for some serious soul-searching, and before long Jonah had become an undone worshipper, rediscovering God, and longing to get right with Him: 'When my life was ebbing away, I remembered you, LORD' (2:7).

Jonah was searched by the spotlight of God's holy love. It's tough being inside a fish for a few days, but it's a whole lot tougher being in a raging ocean. God put Jonah through the refining fire, and he came out of it a stronger, purer worshipper: 'But I, with a song of thanksgiving, will sacrifice to you. What I have vowed I will make good' (2:9).

And just as Isaiah's encounter with God gave him the desire to go out and speak the word, so, too, Jonah set out again—this time on the road to Nineveh. Sometimes we, too, find we've strayed off course, and God has to shake us up to get us back on the right path. He'll often bring us into a season of brokenness, a time to refocus and check that we are heading in the right direction.

A few years ago, I found myself in one of those seasons. We'd been busy recording an album of new worship songs and were trying to fit in a few ministry trips as well. One Friday, after playing guitar all week, I headed off to Holland for a couple of Soul Survivor events. Carrying my guitar to the plane, I noticed my arm was starting to ache. 'Just tiredness,' I thought. But during the weekend, it became more painful every time I played. By the day we left, I was starting to get a bit worried. I got some pretty unhelpful medical advice, then my whole arm started to swell up, and even the slightest movement was agony. 'What's happening, Lord? We've got an album to finish—I can't afford for this to happen now.' Then my hand started to freeze up too.

A week later, through some amazing twists and turns of God's provision, I found myself sitting in the surgery of a top hand specialist. He confirmed that I had a very acute form of tendinitis and said that if he hadn't seen me then, my hand may have been damaged permanently. It was a terrifying moment.

For the next seven weeks I could do hardly anything, and most frustrating of all, I couldn't play my guitar. I sat at home with loads of questions buzzing round in my head. Why was this happening? Would my arm ever fully recover? Was it the devil? Or was it God? I didn't really have any theological answers; but I soon realised that, whatever the answer to those questions, God was at work in the situation. He started speaking to me: as a servant I was dispensable—servants come and go, and God can choose any of us to do any job in His Kingdom. As a worship leader I was replaceable—God could have used anyone for the events that we'd been privileged to be a part of. But as a son, and as a child of God, I was indispensable. There could never be another me—a child is irreplaceable. I was starting to get a better perspective of how I should live my life.

I'd spent so many years leading worship that I'd lost the plot a bit, and God was giving me a 'pit stop'; a chance to have some long overdue work done on my heart. He was teaching me once again what it means to be an undone worshipper. When the seven weeks were up, and my arm was better, I realised just how much God had used that season to bless me with His loving discipline. As François Fenelon, a French Christian from the eighteenth century, wrote: 'All our falls are useful if they strip us of a disastrous confidence in ourselves, while they do not take away a humble and saving trust in God.'[2]

God undoes us in many different ways: through situations around us, through a glimpse of His glory, or simply by speaking into a situation when we've made a mess of things. But He never leaves us that way for long: 'Weeping may remain for a night, but rejoicing comes in the morning' (Psalm 30:5). So often God's hand of discipline in our lives is swiftly followed by His hand of tenderness. In Isaiah 40, God's people find that to be true. After a string of harsh rebukes at the end of chapter 39 comes a gentle, refreshing word: 'Comfort, comfort my people, says your God. Speak tenderly to Jerusalem, and proclaim to her that her hard service has been completed' (Isaiah 40:1–2).

Sometimes, though, we are left 'walking with a limp.' We journey into a new season, yet God leaves behind a reminder of the work

He's done in us. The apostle Paul was walking with a limp or, as he described it, a 'thorn in the flesh,' which he pleaded to have removed. But God made it clear that it was a reminder of weakness, and soon Paul himself came to see it as something that kept him from becoming proud (2 Corinthians 12:7–9).

Occasionally my tendinitis still flares up, and in fact it's sore today as I type this. The doctors have said I'll always be prone to it. Perhaps one day I will be fully healed—I really hope so—but for now, every time it troubles me I'm reminded of all that God spoke to me in that situation. It's an invitation to return to my knees and to remain an undone worshipper.

3
the undignified worshipper

The great thing about writing worship songs is that you can plagiarise the Bible, and instead of getting sued, you actually get encouraged! A few years back I wrote a song called 'Undignified.' When I say I wrote it, all I really did was to steal a line King David had come up with a few thousand years before. They were finally bringing the Ark of the Lord back to Jerusalem, and David got pretty excited and danced like a madman. His wife, Michal, despised him for it, and he came out with the now classic line, 'I will celebrate before the LORD. I will become even more undignified than this, and I will be humiliated in my own eyes' (2 Samuel 6:21–22).

What strikes me most about this is the context of David's celebration. He wasn't just one of the crowd at this event—he was the king. Here was a man of great stature, with a public image to protect; a man trusted with more power, authority and wealth than we could ever imagine. Yet he led the way, 'losing' himself so publicly in his worship of God and so on fire with praise that it burned right through any inhibitions or pride. True worship always forgets itself.

One of the Hebrew words for praise, '*Hallal,*' means to be 'clamorously foolish' or 'mad' before the Lord. (That's where we get our word 'Hallelujah' from.) In a 'reasons to be passionate' competition, the church of God should come an easy first, yet too often we find ourselves lagging way behind in this area. Isn't it time we saw a bit more holy mayhem in our worship?

I'm pretty guilty of this myself, to be honest. I could blame it on my personality, but deep down I know that isn't the whole story. Now and again comes a glimpse of a greater freedom in worship. One night, when I was fifteen years old, we were having our normal Friday-night youth meeting. But during the songs of worship God really got hold of my heart in a fresh way, and I felt I could explode with love for Him. I was desperate to somehow let this worship out, but singing didn't feel enough, and I've never really got on with dancing, so it didn't occur to me that was a viable option either! Becoming frantic for a way of releasing my worship, I hurried out of church, forgetting to put my shoes on, and ran round the car park for ten minutes. I must have looked like an idiot. But at the time I couldn't have cared less. I wasn't bothered who saw me or how weird it all looked—I was before God and God alone. As Oswald Chambers said, 'The consequence of abandonment never enters into our outlook, because our lives are so taken up with Him.'[1]

We get so caught up in love and wonder that we forget what others might think and throw ourselves into God's pleasure. I long for more of those times—seasons where my heart is so consumed with Jesus that abandoned worship floods out in extreme ways.

Sometimes we may need reminding how passionate God is for *us*. Jesus' story of the Prodigal Son has to be one of the best pictures of God's passionate heart. The father welcoming his wayward son home is powerful in itself, but the way in which he welcomes him is even more moving. This wealthy, dignified man loses all reserve, running towards his son with complete abandon. This was not the way for a man of his stature to behave; if there was any running to be done, he would always send a servant to do it. But as he races towards his son, we see a powerful picture of abandoned, extravagant love. Our heavenly Father loves us with the same great abandon, and passionate, undignified worship is our only reasonable response.

William Barclay once wrote,

> Love does not stop nicely to calculate the less or more; love does not stop to work out how little it can respectably give. With a kind of divine extravagance love gives everything it has, and never counts the cost. Calculation is never any part of love.[2]

During a big Soul Survivor mission in Manchester, we saw many touching examples of all-out service and devotion. Financially it was a real stretch, and an offering was taken to try and cover some of the costs. One young lady handed in a cheque for a bizarrely precise amount—something like £4,521.02. As well as being deeply moving, this offering also struck us as odd. What a weird amount to give! We later found out that she had emptied the entire contents of her building society account as an act of worship to God.

That young lady's example sums up the heart of undignified worshippers. So completely caught up with God, they spend themselves on Him without a second thought. She didn't stop to calculate the cost or spend days weighing up the pros and cons of her action. But in an undignified—some would say 'foolish'—moment, she gladly gave all she had. God loves the extravagance of a cheerful worshipper.

Another example of an extravagant worshipper was Charles Wesley. Within the space of fifty years, this undignified lover of God wrote around 6,500 songs of praise. One of his earliest ones, written to mark the first anniversary of becoming a Christian, was 'O for a thousand tongues to sing my great Redeemer's praise.' When I first heard this hymn I thought to myself, 'A thousand people singing to God isn't really all that impressive. After all, we've probably all been in meetings bigger than that.' But then I discovered what Wesley was really imagining. He was picturing himself having a thousand tongues! He was saying, 'I wish I had a thousand tongues, because if I did I'd praise God with every single one of them.' In one sense utter foolishness, yet a beautiful picture of extreme worship.

I'm convinced that we're meant to have a bit more of that foolish streak in us—an intense, almost over-the-top edge to our lives and offerings. I've been a Christian for most of my life, and as I grow older, one of the things I'm most scared of is losing that edge. Life rolls on, and we find ourselves with more pressures, responsibilities and distractions. But the key is to somehow keep a vibrant heart, abandoned to God. Would I still run round that car park today? Or would I stop to put my shoes on first and then decide against it altogether 'in case someone sees'?

Going back to that day in Jerusalem, the dancing King David was totally consumed with God and unaware of himself. He didn't care who was watching or what they might think. He was an adoring heart, worshipping with all his might. In Luke 6:45 Jesus said, 'Out of the abundance of the heart his mouth speaks' (NKJV).

And so, too, out of what's stored up in our hearts we sing and serve and live. That's what King David's frenzied dancing was all about. It wasn't a show, nor was it just adrenalin or hype. It was an overflow of the abundance of love for God that was in his heart.

And this is a valuable lesson for us in our worship. In the midst of the madness and energy, we must always make sure it's simply the abundance of our hearts for Jesus, and never a show for the benefit of others. Worship leaders, take note of that. It's all too easy for what was once a pure act out of the abundance of the heart to become more of a performance when we're on a stage in front of others. We need to guard against elements of performance creeping in when we're leading people before the heavenly throne. God has enough beauty, majesty and glory to inspire us for all eternity, so we don't really need the worship leader trying to impress us or hype up some praise. In fact, it's an offence to distract attention from God, and people usually know in their hearts when that's happened. Worship leaders must point as sensitively as possible to the Lord and never to themselves.

I often define good worship leaders as those who lead strongly enough so that people follow, but not so strongly that they themselves become the focus. If you think about it, worship leaders who end up with a whole lot of attention aren't actually very good at their job. It's as simple as that. They are not achieving their ultimate goal.

There's an old hymn that talks of a place, 'when in our music God is glorified, and adoration leaves no room for pride.'[3]

God's throne room allows no room for the proud. If we're to usher others into that place of holy beholding, we need to make sure there's nothing in us that, deep down, still wants to be the centre of attention. He must increase, and we must decrease. He must become greater, and we must become less.

O God, bring us to that place—worshippers and worship leaders alike—where we're so caught up in loving You that we care very little about our own status or reputation. Where we so find You in worship, that we lose ourselves in Your wonder, love and praise.

4
the unpredictable worshipper

It was the week leading up to the cross, and the strain was taking its toll on Jesus. Surrounded by harsh, negative attitudes and awaiting betrayal, the pressure intensified every day. Soon to come was the agony of Gethsemane and Golgotha. Yet in the midst of this torment came a beautiful act, 'an oasis of sweetness in the desert of bitterness.'[1]

Jesus was at the home of a man called Simon, when suddenly a woman carrying a jar of perfume entered the room. Without any explanation, she broke the top off and unashamedly poured the whole jar of perfume over the head of Jesus. It was a crazy thing to do, and everyone there knew it. For one thing, it was an extravagant waste of money. This perfume was meant to be measured out drop by drop, not used all at once. But Jesus didn't see it that way: 'She has done a beautiful thing to me' (Mark 14:6).

For Him, it was a well-timed act of devotion—unexpected, unusual and yet so meaningful to the Son of God. It was the act of a woman who had not been tamed by cynical religious attitudes. She came across them that day but was unaffected by them. It was the worship of a woman who didn't know 'the rules.' An unpredictable, untamed heart on a quest to see Jesus glorified.

As worshippers of Jesus today, we also need to cultivate this sort of unpredictability in our worship. When we come before the Living God, there should always be aspects of the fresh and the surprising. These things are a sign of life. Worship is meant to be an encounter, an exciting meeting place where love is given and received in an unscripted manner. As Gary Furr and Milburn Price put it: 'Because worship is a conversation, and not a mere review of the past, it is dynamic, unpredictable, and open-ended.'[2]

Of course it's right for some worship to follow the same form; traditions arise in every stream of the church, and that's no bad thing. God often chooses to work that way. Elements of the familiar can also be reassuring for the worshipper. But tradition alone can become lifeless, existing to please itself, and leaving no room for spontaneous love. When we meet to worship God, structure, though important, must never be allowed to strangle life. And religion must never be allowed to dampen romance. G. K. Chesterton worried that 'sometimes our worship is more of a theory than a love affair,' and he may have had a point.

God has won the heart of His bride, the church. And it's not meant to be a dry, predictable relationship. It's a 'divine romance,'[3] full of life and energy. True romance is never predictable. It cannot contain its instinctive responses to the one it adores. The romantic heart seeks out new and creative ways of reaching the one it beats for. People in love do lots of crazy things. Sometimes they even become an embarrassment to those around them. The woman who came to Jesus that day with her jar of perfume was probably an embarrassment to every single person in the room. Except, of course, to Jesus.

Isn't it time the bride of Christ did a few more crazy things for the One she loves? In Revelation 2, Jesus tells us that He longs for the church to do the things she did at first. The church in Ephesus, to whom He's speaking, seems out of love. She is enduring hardship, yet no longer enjoying Jesus. What sort of relationship is that—enduring it but not enjoying it anymore? Where is the first love this church once knew? Where is the romance that once dreamt up imaginative ways of showing adoration?

The cynic may say it's just a fact of life and that this kind of downfall is inevitable. Sometimes the cynic in me says the same. I think back to some high watermarks in my life with God; times when my heart seemed more ready to adore God in unpredictable, crazy ways. I didn't care what religious environment I was in. I was ready to break the top off the alabaster jar and pour out the perfume unsparingly. But now I sometimes find myself rationing out the oil of my love for God, drop by drop, with no passion or spontaneity, afraid to follow the unpredictable in case it seems too unusual or out of place. And I'm meant to be a worship leader!

But in my spirit I know a relationship with the Living God shouldn't just fade away or wear out like an old pair of shoes. It's meant to be new every morning, just like the mercy it responds to. In my heart, and more importantly in God's heart, there's a call to return to the first love, the place of romance in worship. This is God's invitation to all of us.

God often calls worship leaders to do the unexpected. Sometimes He has a particular provision for a particular moment. If we do what the Father is doing, when He's doing it, God will break into our services in powerful and surprising ways. That's the key to all effective ministry—to do what the Father is doing, exactly at the right time.

Several years back, Mike Pilavachi and I were invited to Norway for a ministry trip. At the time, Mike had a fear of flying, and he insisted we take the ferry instead of the plane. So unfortunately, what would have been a mere forty-minute trip to the airport and a ninety-minute flight, turned into a six-hour drive to the ferry, followed by a twenty-six-hour sea crossing. (Not that I'm still bitter!) Adding to my nightmare, the only thing to do on the ferry was play bingo, so we were in for a very boring trip. To cut a long (and I mean long) story short I arrived in Norway in a very bad mood.

Finally we arrived at the youth meeting. It was one of those tough meetings, where everything seemed a struggle. I tried lots of different approaches, but nothing seemed to cut through. Everything bombed, no one really entered in, and I felt myself sinking.

Suddenly a song entered my mind. But it wasn't the sort of thing I was wanting to hear at that moment. Instead of hearing a fresh, spontaneous line that would miraculously draw everyone together in worship, all I could think of was the Michael Jackson song 'You are not alone,' which was currently in the charts. I thought I sensed a little whisper telling me to sing this song next in the worship time. 'I'm not doing that!' I said to myself, and was embarrassed that I'd even thought it. But it wouldn't go away, and I soon faced up to the fact that actually things could only get better, and not worse. So against all my better judgements, I launched myself into the chorus of this song, struggling to guess the chords as I went along: 'You are not alone, I am here with you …'[4]

It was a terrifying moment. The minute I started the song I thought, 'What are you doing, you idiot? You're meant to be leading worship, not doing cheesy acoustic cover versions!' I can only imagine that's what it feels like to walk a tightrope. Once you've started walking, there's no way out of it, and the only thing to do is keep on going and not look down. So I shut my eyes, hoped for the best, and wondered when the next ferry home was.

After the meeting, when I was head down and packing up my guitars, a group of teenagers came up to me. As it turned out, they weren't Christians, and the Michael Jackson song had been the only entry point into the meeting for them. We ended up playing through some other pop songs together and had a bit of a chat. By the end of our few minutes together I could see their attitude to church had changed a bit. 'Thank You, Lord,' I thought. 'At least something good has come out of this.' As they were leaving, out of the corner of my eye I saw a lady coming up to me in tears. I stopped to speak to her, and as she told me her story, I soon realised that God had been working all along. 'I came to this meeting tonight in a terrible state. I've travelled six hours to get here, all the way crying out to God, "Why have You left me all alone? God, You've left me alone, and I'm desperate. I'm going to this meeting as a last resort—I need to hear from You and know that I'm not alone."'

As I'd sung out that song, 'You are not alone, I am here with you,' this lady had broken down in tears. God was answering her desperate prayers in a very direct, personal way.

This isn't the sort of story that happens to me very often, but it served as a good reminder. We must always leave room for the unpredictable in our worship. Sometimes God, in His wisdom, will step in powerfully, through what may seem like foolishness to us.

As a worship leader it can be so easy to get into following a certain routine or formula. There's nothing wrong with planning or having a guide by which you choose songs. In fact, that's really important. But let's also leave room for the romance. Have space in your mind-set for the whisperings of the Holy Spirit to lead you somewhere fresh at any time. As Cardinal Suenens once said: 'The Spirit of God can breathe through what is predicted at a human level with a sunshine of surprises.'[5]

There's nothing more exciting than a dynamic worship time where God breaks in with such a freshness that no one really knows where we're going next. The Holy Spirit will take us into the most wonderful depths of the throne room, and sometimes He will take us there on a route we've never journeyed on before.

That's not to say worship leaders always need to behave unpredictably. That would be stupid. If we did, everyone would soon become irritated and tired of trying to keep up. C. S. Lewis thought that too many new and unpredictable moments in a worship service could end up leaving people focusing on the worship, rather than actually worshipping. Or, if you like, fixing their eyes on the service instead of Jesus. He reminds worship leaders: 'The charge to Peter was Feed my sheep, not Try experiments on my rats, or even, Teach my performing dog new tricks'![6]

The key is to somehow find the right balance between the prophetic (the desire to break new ground) and the pastoral (the desire to take people with us). We need to ask the Holy Spirit to give us the insights and the wisdom to do this.

I recently heard someone use the phrase 'lead worshippers' instead of 'worship leaders.' My immediate reaction, to be honest, was 'Yes, very clever—a cunning play on words.' But the more I've thought about it, the more I'm realising that little twist is actually a very helpful way of looking at things. There's a very real sense in which the Holy Spirit is ultimately the 'worship leader'—He is the agent of everything meaningful that happens in our worship times. Philippians 3:3 tells us that we 'worship by the Spirit of God,' and Jesus points out that a major role of the Holy Spirit is to bring glory to Him. The human 'worship leaders' then become more of 'lead worshippers': trying to follow the leadings of the Holy Spirit, and throwing themselves wholeheartedly into worship as an example for others to follow.

This way of looking at things has some huge implications for worship leaders, or as we're calling them here, lead worshippers. First it can take the pressure off—it reinforces the fact that we can't *make* worship happen. No amount of striving or hyping can communicate real worship. We always worship by the Spirit of God.

The second implication for lead worshippers is that it keeps us dependent. Oswald Chambers once said, 'Complete weakness and our dependence upon Him will be the very moment that the Spirit of God will exhibit His power.'[7] This is a real lesson for those of us involved in leading worship. We hear so much about the practical and external side of things: how to link songs, how to play well and excellence in worship. Don't get me wrong—lots of this stuff is vital. But the key is in remembering there can never be a substitute for the Holy Spirit of God. If He's not involved, we'll know it, and no amount of good musicianship or skilful arrangements will ever be able to fill that gap. I've had the privilege of playing with some fantastic musicians in worship. Even at our home church we are blessed with an abundance of skilful musicians, and now and again I find myself relying too heavily on that, and assuming that if I get a good band together we'll have 'good worship.' But God soon finds a way of reminding me that dependence on Him is, and always will be, the key. Worship is a spiritual event long before it is ever a musical event.

The third implication of this way of looking at things is that not all worship has to originate from the stage. It can be a really helpful model to have a lead worshipper at the front—someone who's invested time in thinking how God might be wanting to lead us and who's picked up some practical skills that mean we can all join in together. But it's also that person's responsibility to be aware that God may want to lead through others, too. It can be so powerful when we create an environment where anyone can feel free to start a song and move in a direction they feel the Holy Spirit is leading. And once again, this takes pressure off those at the front. Many times I've not had a clue what to do next, and then something wonderful has started up from within the congregation.

Sometimes we fall into the trap of forgetting who the Holy Spirit really is. Certain sections of the church try to ignore Him, while others become so over familiar that we even make jokes about the way He meets with us. Perhaps we need to be reminded, in the words of the Nicene Creed, that 'with the Father and the Son [He] is worshipped and glorified.' And we also need to realise that dependence on the Holy Spirit is the key to all authentic worship. As worshippers and worship leaders alike, we must reverence Him more, and rely on Him more.

God is seeking worshippers who will be ready to follow the adventurous whispers of His Holy Spirit, the true 'worship leader.' People who, with their lives, and when they gather together, keep alive the romance of the first love—with hearts that are always ready for the unpredictable.

5
the unveiled worshipper

At the end of Exodus 34, Moses came down from Mount Sinai after a powerful encounter with the Living God. He'd been ushered into an incredible level of revelation—so deep into the heart of God's glory that his face was actually shining. So radiant, in fact, that the people were afraid even to look at him. From that time on, Moses wore a veil to cover up his face. But 'whenever he entered the LORD's presence to speak with him, he removed the veil until he came out' (v. 34).

When he went to meet with God, nothing, not even a layer of cloth, would be allowed to hinder his gaze upon God.

That passage gives us insight into two things: the deep revelation of God, and the change it brings to those who experience it. And the greater the revelation, the greater the transformation. Unveiled in his worship and given incredible access to the presence of God, Moses also became a changed worshipper, glowing with the glory of God.

The New Testament has amazing news for us—we, too, can be unveiled worshippers: 'And we, who with unveiled faces all reflect the Lord's glory, are being transformed into his likeness with ever-increasing glory, which comes from the Lord, who is the Spirit' (2 Corinthians 3:18).

God has invited us into an incredibly privileged place in worship. In one sense, the Almighty need not reveal Himself to anyone. He is a consuming fire, blazing with power and holiness. And yet He burns with a heart of love for His people, longing to usher each one of us into deeper levels of glory. It's there we are transformed ever more into His likeness. As someone once put it, 'beholding is becoming.'

When I was seven years old, my dad died suddenly. One day he was with us, and the next day gone. I found out a few years later that he'd actually committed suicide. That discovery brought new pain and new questions. Was it my fault? Did he not love me enough to stay alive? My mum remarried, and what seemed at first to be another chance to have a father soon turned sour. He messed things up and then left.

But in the middle of all this, God was on my case. The Psalms tell us He's a 'Father to the fatherless,' and as I drew close to Him, I found healing in my heavenly Father's arms. I'm sure the main way this happened was in times of worship. I'd find myself weeping, sometimes for no obvious reason. But as I look back now, I see that God was making my heart tender and drawing out the painful wounds of the past. I didn't go to get healed—I went because God had captured my heart. But you can never outgive the true Giver. All the time, there was me thinking I was bringing Him something! Yet God, in His mercy, had other plans. I was an unveiled worshipper being transformed in His presence. Every time I drew near, I came down the mountain a little more whole and a little bit more like Him.

The Bible clearly shows that God wants His people to have a close encounter with Him. When Jesus came to earth, His words, life and death brought a fresh invitation to draw near to the Almighty. He taught His disciples to pray to an intimate Father in heaven, just as He did. He said they were no longer just servants, but friends, for everything He'd learned from the Father He was showing to them. In Revelation 3:20 Jesus reminded the Laodicean church of this invitation: 'Here I am! I stand at the door and knock. If anyone hears my voice and opens the door, I will come in and eat with him, and he with me.'

Often we take this to be an evangelistic passage, yet really Jesus was talking to people who were already following Him. He was inviting His people to a greater intimacy.

The word for 'eat' here is taken from the Greek noun '*deipnon*,' which described the main meal of the day. It was the evening meal, where people would sit down together at the end of a day's work and spend quality time with one another. In that culture the reason for such a meal was fellowship and not just food. It wasn't a hurried event, but one where you'd sit for a while and get to know those you ate with. Jesus was saying, in effect, 'Let Me deeper into your life. I want to come and eat with you, to be close to you. I am not calling you just to be a waiter at the table, serving Me as I eat. I'm calling you to sit down with Me, and for us to eat together.'

This is the same Jesus who, two chapters earlier, is described as having eyes of fire and a face shining like the sun in all its brightness. Intimate as it may be, this will never be a meal between two equals.

We know we're not worthy to so much as gather up the crumbs under His table, but that is the beauty of it. The invitation Jesus gives us is surely the greatest mystery of the universe. Fascinating as it would be to know exactly how the earth was formed, or how far the star-filled galaxies stretch, I'm far more captured by this mystery—that Almighty God would invite me to intimacy with Himself, and that the Son of God would willingly die on a cross to make that possible.

Far from competing with each other, intimacy and reverence actually go hand in hand. The Bible tells us that 'the friendship of the LORD is for those who fear him' (Psalm 25:14 NRSV). When the fear of the Lord meets the friendship, that's when this mystery really kicks in. How can it be that the eternal God would beckon someone like me into His everlasting arms?

The first chapter of Revelation gives us a powerful picture of intimacy meeting reverence. The writer, John, has an amazing encounter with the Lord. In verse 16, Jesus is described as an awe-inspiring being who holds the seven stars in His right hand. Yet in the very next verse we're told that Jesus then placed this same right hand on John and comforted him, urging him not to be afraid. It's a picture of awe and yet intimacy. William Barclay summed it up perfectly: 'The hand of Christ is strong enough to uphold the heavens and gentle enough to wipe away our tears.'[1]

This fusion of friendship and fear is also found in the life of Job. He's an interesting case study of how a worshipper came to know something of the 'otherness' of God. Under intense suffering, Job looked back, pining for the days 'when God's intimate friendship blessed my house' (Job 29:4). He'd known the friendship of the Lord. But at the end of his ordeal Job had come to know God in a new way. Aspects of God's power and greatness were unveiled which Job had never truly recognised before. As Job himself put it, 'My ears had heard of you but now my eyes have seen you' (Job 42:5).

The revelation of God crashed right through into his heart. And he realised more than ever the wonder of the Almighty. We're told that God blessed the latter part of Job's life more than the first. That's talking about his family and wealth, but surely it must also mean that this sense of God's intimate friendship returned in abundance. Job was a man who came to know an increasing measure of both the friendship and the fear of the Lord. And, as such, he was a man transformed by the revelation of God.

Several years back I was invited to Buckingham Palace for a function hosted by the Queen and Prince Charles. Not that I'd done anything to deserve going, but a friend of mine was asked to nominate a couple of young Christians and thought it would be pretty funny to send me! To be honest I'm not one for these grand occasions—I'm a 'jeans' man, and it's not often you'll see me wearing proper trousers, let alone a suit. But on this occasion I knew that preparing to meet the Queen meant a little more than my usual 'Is this T-shirt clean?' routine which I go through most mornings. I needed to prepare myself properly, and that meant dressing up smartly.

How much more then should we prepare our hearts when we come to meet with Almighty God? I'm not suggesting we dress up every Sunday in our smartest outfit (though if you like to, fantastic). But I am suggesting we need to take a bit more care in our approach to the Almighty. The Creator of the universe has opened a door to closeness with Him, and we need to ensure we never take it for granted. If this talk of intimacy is to be wholesome, we must never forget who it is we are approaching. The writer of Ecclesiastes put it perfectly:

> Guard your steps when you go to the house of God.... Do not be quick with your mouth, do not be hasty in your heart to utter anything before God. God is in heaven and you are on earth, so let your words be few. (Ecclesiastes 5:1–2)

In the previous chapter we talked about times when it's good to let our hearts overflow abundantly and even wildly. But there's also a time to be still, and just to know that God is God. A time to reflect on who He is and respond with the fewest of words and the simplest of songs. As the Ecclesiastes passage goes on to say, 'Therefore stand in awe of God' (v. 7).

And sometimes, we don't even get to stand. I've been struck recently by how many times people in the Bible encounter God and end up on their knees. We've already visited the passage in Revelation 1 where John encounters the glorious Jesus and falls at His feet 'as though dead.' Three chapters later, the twenty-four elders are falling down before God too, and worshipping Him. Psalm 72:11 tells us that 'all kings shall fall down before him' (KJV), and we know of course that one day every knee will bow.

For me, though, one of the most striking pictures of all is seen in the Garden of Gethsemane. An outsider might argue that Jesus was at His least powerful there. Many were plotting against Him, and He knew He was soon to be betrayed. The cross cruelly awaited Him. So pressured was the Son of God that His sweat was like 'drops of blood falling to the ground' (Luke 22:44). Judas, some Pharisees, chief priests, and a detachment of soldiers arrived to arrest Him. They were even carrying weapons. But then something incredible happened:

> Jesus, knowing all that was going to happen to him, went out and asked them, 'Who is it you want?' 'Jesus of Nazareth,' they replied … *When Jesus said 'I am he,' they drew back and fell to the ground.* (John 18:4–5, author's paraphrase)

This amazes me. There in the Garden of Gethsemane the man Jesus was weary, troubled and unarmed. Yet even in this moment, a mark of His ultimate identity shines through. These aggressive, unyielding soldiers, priests and Pharisees were somehow compelled to bow the knee, if only for a moment. How much more then should we, as yielding worshippers of the crucified, risen and ascended Jesus, seek out some floor space.

When we really pay attention to God's worth, our worship times will start to look even more like the heavenly throne room. The angels sing, as do we. The living creatures speak out their praise, and we join them. But the twenty-four elders bow down on their faces. Oh that we would see what they see, and do as they do, a little more often. To bow is the ultimate physical sign of reverence.

There's definitely a different dynamic in worship that kicks in when we truly take our eyes off ourselves and fix them firmly on Jesus. I worry that too often we spend our worship times reflecting on how we are doing and what we have gained. As Anthony Bloom once said, 'So often when we say "I love you" we say it with a huge "I" and a small "you."'[2]

But there's a wonderful, biblical dynamic in worship when we lift our eyes off ourselves and gaze upon the beauty of God. William Barclay describes just how a heart captured by the wonder of Jesus gazes upon Him:

> He looks with wondering amazement; he looks as one who looks to a champion and a saviour … he looks as … one looks with adoration at his lover … he looks … to God when God has become for him the only reality in the world.[3]

In an age of informality and irreverence, true unveiled worshippers recognise the 'otherness' of God and treasure the call to intimacy with Him. Transfixed by His glory and transformed in His presence, we become ever more like Him. Unveiled worshippers come down the mountain different. They are radiant, for all to see, shining with the glory of God.

6
the unstoppable worshipper

The year is 1744, and hymn writer Charles Wesley is in Leeds, holding a prayer meeting in an upstairs room. Suddenly there's a creak in the floorboards, followed by a massive crack, and the whole floor collapses. All one hundred people crash right through the ceiling into the room below. The place is in chaos—some are screaming, some are crying, some just sit in shock. But as the dust settles, Wesley, wounded and lying in a heap, cries out, 'Fear not! The Lord is with us. Our lives are all safe.' And then he breaks out into the Doxology: 'Praise God, from whom all blessings flow.' Perhaps a bizarre choice of song, considering what's just happened! But there's the point—while everyone else was still licking their wounds, the heart of this unstoppable worshipper was responding with unshakeable praise.[1]

Unstoppable worshippers will never quit when it comes to adoring God. Faced with opposition, danger or even death they just keep going. We're told of worshippers in the early church who, more than simply enduring, actually rejoiced 'because they had been counted worthy of suffering disgrace for the Name' (Acts 5:41).

True worship often meets with opposition. Take the life of David. His first triumph was a powerful public act of unstoppable worship. The giant Goliath had put fear into all Israel, and the whole nation was afraid to stand up against him for the honour of God's name. Then in walked David—too small for a suit of armour, and as Saul told him, still only a boy. Yet this passionate lover of God couldn't stand to see the armies of the Living God made a fool of, and he walked out onto that battlefield so 'the whole world will know that there is a God in Israel' (1 Samuel 17:46). Goliath looked him over and despised him (v. 42), but, anointed by God and driven by passion for Him, David overcame. The worship of God won the day.

That wasn't the only time David was despised for being a worshipper. In the undignified episode when David danced before God with all his might, his own wife despised him. To the heart of God it was a beautiful act of worship. But in the eyes of Michal it was a complete embarrassment (2 Samuel 6:16). And she wasn't the only one in David's family who despised his passion for God. Check out Psalm 69:

> Those who hate me without reason outnumber the hairs of my head ... For I endure scorn for your sake, and shame covers my face. I am a stranger to my brothers, an alien to my own mother's sons; *for zeal for your house consumes me*, and the insults of those who insult you fall on me. (Psalm 69:4, 7–9)

The giant Goliath was perhaps an obvious enemy to David's worship of God, the sort of opposition you'd expect when you stand up on a battlefield for the honour of God's name. But the opposition from within his own family was very different, and one which I'm sure he would have found even harder to overcome.

Dietrich Bonhoeffer, a Christian in Germany at the time of the Second World War, once said: 'When Christ calls a man he bids him come and die.'[2]

Obviously he was talking of dying to self—taking up our cross, denying ourselves and following Jesus. But for Bonhoeffer himself it turned out to have a much more literal meaning. At the age of thirty-nine, very close to the end of the war, he was taken out of prison and hanged for his courageous stand against Hitler and the Nazi party. As he left his cell, he said, 'This is the end—but for me, the beginning of life.'[3] They could kill his body, but they could not stop his worship.

Unstoppable worshippers are bold evangelists, lifting up the name of Jesus everywhere they get the chance. Their offerings of worship are just as vibrant outside the walls of the church as they are inside. They are adventurous hearts, taking every opportunity to demonstrate the good news of God to this world. In chains for doing just that, the apostle Paul urged the church in Ephesus:

> Pray also for me, that whenever I open my mouth, words may be given me so that I will fearlessly make known the mystery of the gospel.... Pray that I may declare it fearlessly, as I should. (Ephesians 6:19–20)

Here was a man in prison again for proclaiming Jesus. His boldness had got him arrested, and common sense would have said, 'Pray that I keep my mouth shut next time.' But instead, he prayed for more boldness! Paul's mission in life was to make his glorious Jesus known, and if that stirred up trouble for him, then so be it.

If the apostle Paul needed to pray for more boldness, how much more do we? I've always found it very easy to lift up Jesus in the context of church, but very hard to find opportunities—and take them—outside. Putting it bluntly, I can be a complete coward! At the age of sixteen I used to wear a 'cross' lapel badge on my school uniform. If I'm honest, I think I was pretty proud of myself; that is, until the day I applied for a Saturday job at my local bike store. Just before the interview, I took the badge off, hiding it away in my pocket, just in case wearing it would ruin my chances of getting the job. In the middle of the interview, I suddenly realised what I'd done, and I felt so ashamed. There I sat with the cross in my pocket, wondering how I could ever be embarrassed of what Jesus had done for me.

The only other job I've ever had is working for the church, and of course I'd have been a lot keener to wear my cross badge for that interview! But isn't that what many of us are like? We'll carry high the cross at church and then hide it away in our pockets when we go out into the rest of life. I learned a real lesson that day. I need to queue up with the apostle Paul for some more Holy Spirit boldness. If I can't even carry a little lapel badge cross, how on earth am I going to manage a real one?

The story of Rachel Scott, a teenage victim of the Columbine High School tragedy, is another powerful tale of unstoppable worship. On 20 April 1999, two bitter and twisted students entered the grounds of a US school with guns and explosives, planning to wreak havoc. One of the grudges they were bearing was against Christians, and when they found Rachel Scott that grudge was made very clear. The killers shot her twice in the legs and once in the upper body. As she struggled to crawl away to safety, they pulled her up by the hair, and asked, 'Do you believe in God?' They thought they'd won the battle, expecting her to back down from her faith with a whimpering 'no.' But this bleeding, unstoppable worshipper bravely affirmed, 'You know I do.' Furious with that answer they yelled, 'Then go be with Him,' and shot her right through the head.[4]

Imagine the heart of God in that moment, as one of His precious worshippers threw her life on the line for His glory. In a gruesome moment of decision, she chose His honour over her own survival. This story stirs my heart up every time I hear it. And if it affects us so much, imagine what effect it must have on the heart of Jesus.

The story of Stephen's stoning in Acts 7 sheds some more light on this. He put his life on the line, proclaiming Jesus to cold hearts that didn't want to hear, and rebuked them for their religious pride. But just before they stoned him to death, God allowed Stephen an amazing depth of revelation—perhaps to help this first Christian martyr stay strong to the end. Stephen was allowed a glimpse of heaven's throne room and saw Jesus 'standing' at the right hand of God. The odd thing here is that Jesus was standing. Every other time in the New Testament we hear of Jesus at the right hand of God, He's sitting down. So why was He standing then?

He may not have been the world's greatest theologian, but I love Smith Wigglesworth's explanation: though usually He is seated at the right hand of God, this time Jesus got to His feet to honour and spur

Stephen on in his courageous act of worship.[5] It's as if He was saying, 'Look up, look up! You have honoured Me today, and forever I will be your very great reward. I am on My feet to spur you on. Look up to Me, look up to Me, for your brave worship has brought honour to My name and pleasure to My heart.'

While walking this earth, Jesus Himself lived out unstoppable acts of devotion to the heart of His Father. The cross, of course, is the ultimate expression of this, but in the week leading up to the crucifixion we find another powerful example. Jesus and His disciples were just finishing the Last Supper, which would have been a Passover meal. In the Passover tradition, a number of hymns were sung, the last of which was Psalm 136, 'The Great Hallel.'[6] Mark's gospel tells us, 'When they had sung a hymn, they went out to the Mount of Olives' (14:26). So it's very likely this hymn was Psalm 136. The psalm begins,

> Give thanks to the LORD, for he is good.
>   *His love endures forever.*
> Give thanks to the God of gods.
>   *His love endures forever.*
> Give thanks to the Lord of lords:
>   *His love endures forever.*
> to him who alone does great wonders,
>   *His love endures forever.*
> who by his understanding made the heavens,
>   *His love endures forever.*
> who spread out the earth upon the waters,
>   *His love endures forever.* (v. 1–6)

The rest of the psalm carries on in much the same way, and by the end of it the phrase 'His love endures forever' has appeared twenty-six times. Think about that for a minute. Judas' betrayal is knocking loudly at the door. The Garden of Gethsemane is beckoning. The shadow of the cross falls right across this meal, and yet Jesus can declare twenty-six times, 'His love endures forever.' That is amazing. Even in this dark, dark hour, His devotion to the Father will not be broken. His heart of worship refuses to be intimidated. Doesn't that teach us something about worship?

Unstoppable worshippers let nothing hinder them in their quest to glorify God. Whatever 'goliaths' come their way, they walk out onto that worship battlefield and take their chances. They do not shrink back in times of trouble, but instead raise a spirited psalm of trust and praise.

7

the unnoticed worshipper

The conductor Leonard Bernstein was once asked, 'What is the most difficult instrument to play?'

'Second violin,' he replied, 'because everyone wants to be first violinist.'

Of course the first violin gets to play more interesting parts, and commands more attention. But, as Bernstein goes on to explain, 'It's hard to find someone who wants to play second violin and to do so with the same enthusiasm. But without the second violin, there is no harmony.'

There's a lesson in here for all of us. So much of what we pay attention to in life happens on a stage of some kind. People like to be noticed, and our culture is in love with celebrity. Some will go to any length to make sure they get some attention. God, on the other hand, has a very different way of looking at things. He might watch the show, but He's much more concerned with what's going on backstage. We so often look at the outward appearance, but God goes straight to the heart. We become consumed with the public side of things, but God is always far more interested in the hidden and the private.

There's a great example of this in Luke 21:1–4. Jesus is watching the rich putting their gifts into the temple treasury, when a little act of hidden worship catches His eye. A poor widow walks up and puts in some tiny copper coins, worth almost nothing in the world's eyes. But Jesus declares, 'This poor widow has put in more than all the others.'

At first that sounds ridiculous, until we understand that Jesus is looking way beyond the coins themselves, right into her heart. He sees that these tiny coins, so gladly given, are all she has to live on. It's a costly, faithful offering of the heart, unnoticed by all around her, except for Jesus, who sees as heaven would.

Unnoticed worshippers are not looking for attention from this world—their offerings are as private as possible. But because of what they bring, and the way they bring it, heaven is paying extra special attention. Unnoticed perhaps by those around them, they do not go unnoticed by the heart of God. Most examples in this book so far have been acts of worship carried out in public. But God seeks first devotion to Him in the hidden place—worship when no one else is watching.

The life of King David gives us some great insight into the balance of public and private in the heart of a worshipper. It seems pretty clear that David grew up knowing the Lord, no doubt offering up many passionate yet unnoticed acts of worship as he spent time alone tending sheep. In fact he was probably only fifteen years old when Samuel described him to Saul as 'a man after [God's] own heart' (1 Samuel 13:14).

But then life got a bit more complicated. David became the most well-known worshipper in the whole of the land. From the Goliath incident onwards, he was involved in some very public acts of devotion. Women even started singing songs about him: 'Saul has slain his thousands, and David his tens of thousands' (1 Samuel 18:7). A few years later David became king.

In the midst of all this, the key for David was to try and maintain the heart of worship he had before life got complicated. In one sense it was easy then—for one thing, he could test his motives pretty simply. Every song he sang, and every prayer he prayed, was truly for an audience of one—no one else was around to witness his love for God in those lonely fields. Then he became a public figure, and from that time on his devotion was out in the open. The test was this: could he preserve that simple, pure heart of adoration in the midst of all the public things he became entrusted with?

And that's the test for all of us. I guess I'm talking more here to worship leaders and musicians than anyone else. The toughest test for our hearts doesn't come 'out in the fields' when there's no one else around. The really hard part begins when we start getting trusted with the public stuff. Maybe that's playing in the worship team at church, or wherever. God calls us to check ruthlessly the motives of our hearts. Do we still want to be unnoticed worshippers now that we're on a stage? Or is there a part of us that really wants to be a 'noticed' worshipper? Are we still happy to serve? Or is there even just a tiny part of us wanting to be served? Are our songs still aimed at an audience of one, or deep down are we starting to want wider acclaim? These are tough questions to face, but they're essential if we're going to stay faithful to the calling God has on our lives.

In the design of a boat, what's below the waterline must always outweigh what's above the waterline. Otherwise, that boat will capsize at the first sign of strong winds. It's the same with our hearts. Things can look impressive on the outside—perhaps we've learnt a few cool guitar licks, or our voices seem stronger than ever. But God's infinitely more concerned with what's going on below the waterline. What are we like when no one else can see us? How much do we throw ourselves into worship at church when we're not leading? Or, even more to the point, when someone else is leading worship in a style not quite to our taste?

And what's going through our minds when we lead? Are there little moments of self-congratulation when things are going well? Again, these are tough questions, but so important if we're going to get this worship thing right and really honour God. The key is to try and keep the public side of things outweighed by the private. As the late John Wimber taught, the real test in these days isn't going to be in the writing and producing of new and great worship music; the real test is going to be in the godliness of those who deliver it.

One trend in worship which increasingly worries me is the whole performance thing. It's been creeping up for years. Somehow we've got to a place where we'll even call worship events a 'gig' or a 'concert'—the danger being that words like those throw us right off the scent of what worship really is. Too many times I've found myself in a meeting where I'm longing to engage with God while struggling to get past the impressive, yet ultimately distracting, show going on up the front. Some may argue that performance can be worship, and that's true. In one way, everything can be worship, if there's a good heart behind it. But performance is not necessarily a good way of *leading* worship. A worship leader needs as much as possible to be the unnoticed worshipper, simply encouraging the worship of God by setting an example for others to follow. To draw attention to ourselves in moments meant for a holy beholding is a pretty unbiblical approach. In fact, it's probably even a dangerous one.

Praise is a contradiction of pride. Pride says 'look at me,' but praise longs for people to see Jesus. There's no room for showing off in the holy throne room. Picture it now: there we stand in the glorious presence of Almighty God, elders bowing as low as they can and seraphs covering their faces. But there's one person—right in the middle of the whole thing—showing off a bit. A little dance routine, an over-the-top vocal, and just generally hamming it up. Ridiculous? Of course. And I've exaggerated to make a point, but I hope the point is clear. It wouldn't hurt to run everything we do in worship through that filter. The reality is that in the throne room of Almighty God, everyone's bowing as low as they can.

In the 1700s a Frenchman called François Fenelon wrote down some great advice for any worship leader: 'Make yourself little in the depths of your heart.'[1] If we truly do this, our actions and attitudes will naturally follow through. If we make sure we're bowing low in our hearts, the chances are that the outward way we lead worship will be more appropriate too. Proverbs 25:6 sums it up: 'Do not exalt yourself in the king's presence.'

At a recent worship leaders' retreat, I believe God gave me a picture to illustrate this entrustment given to worship leaders. I saw a young man on a journey. He has been entrusted with the most beautiful jewel. Yet this treasure is not for him—he is on a mission to bring it before his king. So precious is the jewel that he hides it away as he travels along the road. Every now and then he stops at a town or village. And that's when the temptations start. It would be so easy to show his treasure off a bit and let people marvel at this wonder he's been entrusted with. It would certainly bring him a lot of fame and favour. He could still take it to the king one day but maybe have some fun along the way. Another temptation is to even settle down in that town, basking in his newfound popularity, and abandon the mission altogether. He could even sell the treasure. If he did, he'd never have to work again.

Every time he's around people, the enticements seem to grow stronger. And yet he remains faithful and resists all these temptations, finally reaching the king's palace. Entering the throne room, with the treasure still intact, he looks up and sees the king. But more than that, he sees the king's pleasure; it is written all over his face.

Worship leaders, we're on a sacred journey. The cargo is precious, and the mission is vital. If we're to really see our King's pleasure in this whole worship music movement, then there are some narrow paths we need to cling to. At times it may seem more attractive to find pleasure from the people. Many of you have a lot of gifting and could certainly impress a lot of people. If you really wanted to, you could grab a whole lot of attention for yourself. But the challenge is this: to stay pure and true to the cause. Always keep in mind the end of the journey—the pleasure of the King over you, as you bring your unspoilt offering before Him, and Him alone.

In many ways, this is a key time for worship leading. When things get exciting, it can be harder to maintain a purity. I came across one songbook recently called something like 'Today's 40 Most Powerful Worship Songs.' A shocking sign of the times. Who told them that?

Was it God? How nice of Him to reveal His forty favourites so that a book could be marketed effectively! I'm being extremely cheeky, and in all truth that same company has put out many wonderful resources, so I'm not picking on them. But it's a reminder to me. Let's test everything we do—every heart attitude, every way we lead worship, every resource we put out under the title of 'worship.'

It's a time to be on our guard—this is a sacred trust. Let's keep our worship pleasing to the Father, centred around the Son, and led by the Spirit, not the flesh.

8
the undivided worshipper

In a potentially hypnotising world, the quest for undivided worshippers is simple—to keep their eyes fixed on Jesus. Simple to define perhaps, but in practice not quite so easy. Our hearts are tugged about in so many different directions. Around every corner are new distractions fighting for our attention—so many things that could deflect our time and energy away from loving God.

The psalmist cried out: 'Give me an undivided heart' (Psalm 86:11). Those five words are probably some of the most important we'll ever pray. Every day we come face-to-face with enticements to leave the highway of holiness and walk on other paths. But for the heart consumed with Jesus, all those persuasions are seen for what they really are: empty and meaningless dead ends.

Looking to the example of Jesus Himself, we find some great inspiration. From beginning to end, the story of Jesus' walk on earth is one of an undivided heart, totally committed to the Father and His will. The Son of God walked the way of the cross, resisting anything and everything that would divert Him from this thorny path.

When Jesus explained to His disciples the suffering that must soon come, Peter tried to dissuade Him: 'Never, Lord! … This shall never happen to you!' (Matthew 16:22).

But Jesus rebuked him, seeing the enemy behind his presumably well-meaning words. Peter messed up again in the Garden of Gethsemane. Desperate to defend Jesus from the mob who'd come to arrest Him, he took a sword and cut off the ear of the high priest's servant. But again, Jesus would not allow Peter to distract Him from the road to the cross: 'Put your sword away! Shall I not drink the cup the Father has given me?' (John 18:11).

And to go the extra mile, He touched the man's ear and healed him. Staring the reality of crucifixion in the face, the Son of God refused to be intimidated. On a quest to please His Father, His was a pure, undivided heart.

One time, outraged by the traders and money-changers in His Father's house, Jesus exploded with devotion. Turning over tables, even driving some of the traders out with a whip, He was a scary mixture of passion and aggression (Mark 11:15–17; John 2:13–17). At first it looks like a pretty over-the-top reaction. Had all the pressure finally got to Him? Had the sinless One suddenly lost all self-control? Where is the meek and mild Jesus we're taught to expect? But then we discover the righteous reasons behind this fiery outburst.

The temple demanded a tax to be paid by every Jewish man, but it could only be paid in certain types of coin. So the money-changers would exchange a traveller's money for the appropriate temple currencies. At first glance, this looks like a friendly service to offer, but in fact they would take a cut for this, and worshippers would have their money changed at a pretty unfair rate. One writer estimates the exchange fee would have cost about half a day's wage.[1] In Jesus' eyes this behaviour was more than just an unjust practice—it was a barrier to worship.

With the traders it was a similar story. Many visitors to the temple would bring thanksgiving offerings to God, usually a dove or a pigeon. You could buy these from anywhere, but if you bought them outside the temple, you'd have to have them passed by an inspector who'd check the quality of the sacrifice. Again, they'd charge for this and usually make sure they found a fault. That way the worshipper would have to buy one of the temple's 'previously inspected' offerings. To add to this injustice, a dove or a pigeon from a temple trader would be hugely overpriced.[2] So again, a money-making scheme, and a huge obstacle to many worshippers, especially the poor.

Furious at the twisting of God-given guidelines for financial gain, Jesus responded in a rage of violent devotion. This 'den of thieves' should have been a 'house of prayer' (Mark 11:17 NKJV). His Father's house had become a greed-infested trading place.

Jesus is the Perfecter of our faith, and true undivided worshippers follow His example. Nothing can distract, dissuade or deter them from their ultimate goal: the glory and pleasure of God. Dying to themselves and living for Him, they boldly join in the prayer of Charles Wesley:

> Let earth no more my heart divide;
> With Christ may I be crucified.[3]

In many ways worship involves both 'defence' and 'attack.' Looking at the above examples, Jesus displayed both types of worship. On the road to the cross, He defended His heart from all those who would deter Him from His chosen path of praise. He had the purest of hearts, casting aside every temptation to water down His mission. Consumed with the honour of God, Jesus stuck unswervingly to the race set before Him, defending His Father's will from every assault.

In the temple courts Jesus was very much in attacking mode. He wrecked the traders' stalls, seeking out every impure practice and destroying it. Nothing should stand in the way of His Father's worship.

As undivided worshippers we're called to do the same. We need to be untainted hearts, defending ourselves from everything that seeks to lead us off the path of pure worship. But also we need to be in attack mode, striking out for the honour of God's name everywhere we find a suitable opportunity. Sometimes that will mean standing up forcibly for God's praise. At other times a simple act of compassion will speak just as loudly and clearly. In James 1:27 we find an example of these two types of worship—'attack' and 'defence'—working together: 'Religion that God our Father accepts as pure and faultless is this: to look after orphans and widows in their distress and to keep oneself from being polluted by the world.'

In the first part of the verse James was urging us to get into attacking mode and live our worship out loud. He was saying to go to the broken and the neglected and please God's heart in that place. But notice also he was talking about playing on the defence: guarding our hearts against the pollution that's all around us in this world.

Sometimes the assaults on our worship are really obvious, and you can see them coming a mile off. But often they are much more subtle, slowly creeping up on us so that we're even unaware we're losing out to them. For me, one of the big ones is 'busyness.' No matter how many times I learn the lesson, I always seem to find myself busying myself with preparations, like Martha did. And I end up neglecting the better thing: to sit at the feet of Jesus devotedly, like Mary (Luke 10:38–42).

Sometimes the things pulling us away from the feet of Jesus are in themselves 'good' things. I'll tell you some of mine: conferences, working on songs, organising worship teams. Surprised? It's ironic, but if we're not careful, even these things can become distractions to our worship, or meaningless replicas of the real thing. Of course it's fine to work hard—that's a great biblical ethic—but there's also a line to be drawn.

From my early teenage years I've more or less grown up in one form of Christian leadership or another. I started off leading a little home group, doing a few poems at the front of church and playing in the worship band. As time went on, I acquired more responsibilities. We planted a church, I went full-time as a worship leader, and we started doing a bit of travelling, too. A couple of years further down the line I started to reflect on where my heart was at. I was tired, I was burdened; but more than anything, I was dry. I came across two lines of a hymn by William Cowper which summed it all up for me:

> Where is the blessedness I knew when first I saw the Lord?
> Where is the soul-refreshing view of Jesus and His word?[4]

In many ways that's still my heart-cry today. I've grown as a Christian in different areas of my life, and I hope that I've matured in my faith. But I know I've let some things slip too. There was a simplicity in my worship back then—the raw, uncomplicated devotion of a fascinated heart. Sometimes I rationalise the whole thing. I tell myself that life can never be the same as it was when I was a relatively carefree teenager with spare time on my hands. After all, everything's much more complicated now. I've got lots of responsibility and a busy job. When I reason like this, it can seem obvious. I couldn't possibly have the same sort of walk with God that I did back then. Or could I? The more I reflect, the more I realise that's actually a lie of the enemy.

I'm convinced that it's possible to work really hard at the tasks God has called us to and still maintain a vibrant, intimate heart relationship with Him. Jesus did. The key is balancing the times of hard work with times of uninterrupted devotion—moments to be still and know that He is God; times when everything else fades into the background as we sit listening devotedly at the feet of our Master. As Richard Foster reminds us, the divine priority will always be 'worship first, service second.'[5] Interestingly, I find that when I regularly make 'quiet times' to meet with God, I also start becoming much more aware of Him in my everyday activities.

If anything in my life consistently damages my relationship with God, then at some point I have to take responsibility and make some changes. There comes a time when no one else can do that for me. So, as well as praying the old prayer, 'Purify my heart,' I've been praying a new one recently: 'Simplify my life.' There seems to be a strong correlation between those two heart-cries. I'm asking God to help me get rid of unnecessary baggage—anything that consistently weighs me down on my spiritual walk with Him.

It's not only on our personal journey with God that we can get cluttered up with distractions. When we come together as congregations, we can just as easily get thrown off course. A few years back in our church, we realised some of the things we thought were helping us in our worship were actually hindering us. They were throwing us off the scent of what it really means to worship.

We had always set aside lots of time in our meetings for worshipping God through music. But it began to dawn on us that we'd lost something. The fire that used to characterise our worship had somehow grown cold. In some ways, everything looked great. We had some wonderful musicians and a good-quality sound system. There were lots of new songs coming through too. But somehow we'd started to rely on these things a little too much, and they'd become distractions. Where once people would enter in no matter what, we'd now wait to see what the band were like first, how good the sound was, or whether we were 'into' the songs chosen.

Mike, the pastor, decided on a pretty drastic course of action: we'd strip everything away for a season, just to see where our hearts were. So the very next Sunday when we turned up at church, there was no sound system to be seen, and no band to lead us. The new approach was simple—we weren't going to lean so hard on those outward things anymore. Mike would say, 'When you come through the doors of the church on Sunday, what are you bringing as your offering to God? What are you going to sacrifice today?'

If I'm honest, at first I was pretty offended by the whole thing. The worship was my job! But as God softened my heart, I started to see His wisdom all over these actions. At first the meetings were a bit awkward: there were long periods of silence, and there wasn't too much singing going on. But we soon began to learn how to bring heart offerings to God without any of the external trappings we'd grown used to. Stripping everything away, we slowly started to rediscover the heart of worship.

After a while, the worship band and the sound system reappeared, but now it was different. The songs of our hearts had caught up with the songs of our lips.

Out of this season, I reflected on where we had come to as a church, and wrote this song:

When the music fades,
All is stripped away,
And I simply come;
Longing just to bring something that's of worth
That will bless Your heart.

I'll bring You more than a song,
For a song in itself
Is not what You have required.
You search much deeper within
Through the way things appear;
You're looking into my heart.

In the chorus I tried to sum up where we were at with worship:

I'm coming back to the heart of worship,
And it's all about You,
All about You, Jesus.
I'm sorry, Lord, for the thing I've made it,
When it's all about You,
All about You, Jesus.[6]

Tozer once talked of a place where we're 'so hopelessly and totally in love with God that the idea of a transfer of affection never even remotely exists.'[7] And that, in the end, is the true mark of an undivided worshipper. A life that has quite simply become 'all about Jesus.'

9
the unsatisfied worshipper

> Lord, since the day I saw You first,
> My soul was satisfied;
> And yet, because I see in part,
> I'm searching, more to find.[1]

As worshippers of Jesus Christ, we live in the tension of the 'now' and the 'not yet.' From the day we received Him, our souls found their destiny and reason. The reality of His love and presence invaded our hearts, and we found fulfilment. The Bible reveals a God who 'satisfies [our] desires with good things' (Psalm 103:5).

But that's not the whole picture. We're also unsatisfied worshippers—a people who see only in part. This side of heaven, we'll always be carrying in our hearts a holy frustration: the inward groan of believers waiting eagerly for 'our adoption as sons, the redemption of our bodies' (Romans 8:23).

Eugene Peterson wrote: 'Worship does not satisfy our hunger for God—it whets our appetite.'[2] The more we see of Jesus, the more we know there's still so much to be seen. The more He touches our lives, the more we realise our desperate need for Him to consume every part of us. Worship often creates just as many questions as answers. Every glimpse of Jesus, wonderful as it is, is just a drop in the ocean. And the more glimpses we have, the more we begin to realise just how vast that ocean is. We are a people ever searching, 'more of Him to find'; adoring hearts on a tough but rewarding journey. One day we'll reach our final destination, but for now every step on our walk with God is just a tiny foretaste of the glorious inheritance that lies ahead.

Sometimes it's encouraging to realise how far we've already come on our journey. At a quayside, people will draw watermarks—reminders of the levels the tides have reached in that place. In the same way, it's so good to reflect on the peaks and troughs in our own journey. When I look back, I begin to see the marks of God's grace all over my life. The further back I look, the more I realise just how much He's been shaping and healing my heart.

I've always found writing lyrics a great way of documenting my walk with God. Reflecting on different songs or poems can really help me retrace my relationship with Him. One song I wrote, called 'The Father's Song'—based on Zephaniah 3:17—talks of the powerful, life-changing song God sings over His people:

> I have heard so many songs,
> Listened to a thousand tongues,
> But there is one that sounds above them all;

The Father's song, the Father's love—
You sung it over me, and for eternity
It's written on my heart.

Heaven's perfect melody,
The Creator's symphony,
You are singing over me
The Father's song.
Heaven's perfect mystery—
The King of Love has sent for me,
And now You're singing over me
The Father's song.[3]

That verse in Zephaniah has always intrigued me. It's an amazing thought—that God Almighty could be rejoicing over me with singing. Yet one evening, sitting there with my guitar, it struck me more than ever before. So much of my life involves music, but that night I realised that the most meaningful song I'll ever come across will be the one my heavenly Father sings over me.

Soon after writing the song, I found a poem I'd written at the age of fifteen. It had a pretty different tone:

Due to certain circumstances and conditions of my heart
I've been starved of the love of a Father in the past,
And it doesn't seem to matter, but inside there's still a thirst
That says 'I want my Daddy,' like a hurting five-year-old.
Due to matters arising and control of situations
I have run from the love of a Father in the past.

And to me it's not so pure, and I find that I'm not sure
If I want that love to seek me and to reach me anyway.
And it doesn't seem to matter, but inside there's still a thirst
That says 'I want my Daddy,' like a hurting five-year-old.

When I look at these two sets of lyrics back to back, it shocks me. I realise just how far God has brought me along the path of healing. It's easy to forget the pain I'd carried around after my largely fatherless upbringing. The voices of hurt that used to echo so loudly around my head have been drowned out by a different sound: the Father's song. When I compare these two watermarks, I'm humbled by God's hand of kindness in my life.

That's not to say I'm a totally whole person now—far from it. I'm an unfinished heart. Now and again I feel twinges of pain from the past. I may never be free of them this side of heaven. I remain an unsatisfied worshipper, limping towards wholeness, yet full of hope and gratitude.

There's also another reason we're likely to remain unsatisfied worshippers in this life. We start to see the world through the eyes of heaven. The more we see God's perfection, the more we realise the imperfection all around us. True worshippers look outwards—noticing the world they live in and longing to make a difference to the injustice, poverty and pain that surround them. A worshipper of Jesus cannot turn a blind eye to these things. Jürgen Moltmann explained it like this:

> Faith, wherever it develops into hope, causes not rest but unrest.… It does not calm the unquiet

> heart, but is itself this unquiet heart in man. Those who hope in Christ can no longer put up with reality as it is, but begin to suffer under it, to contradict it. Peace with God means conflict with the world.[4]

There's a holy, sometimes painful, frustration that cuts right to the heart of the unsatisfied worshipper. Everything in us knows 'it wasn't meant to be this way.'[5] We become intercessors—people who see the gap and long to stand in it. God imparts to us His heart for restoration and a burning desire to see His love and justice healing the nations. But if we're really to have integrity in our worship, somewhere along the line this desire has to turn into actions: to share our food with the hungry, to clothe the naked and to satisfy the needs of the oppressed (Isaiah 58:7, 10). We cannot be worshippers who simply walk by, ignoring the realities of this broken world. God longs to bring us to the place where we ache so much with His heart, that to do nothing is simply no longer an option.

I've been challenged on this a lot recently. I say I'm a worship leader, and I also say that worship is far more than just about music. So why are all my acts of worship leading done through music? When it comes to reaching the broken of this world, why am I so often near the back of the queue? I'm longing to be a worshipper who sets an example for others to follow, not just with my lips, but with my life. God has made it very clear that worship and justice are inseparable.

To bring it all together, there are three unresolved tensions in the heart of unsatisfied worshippers. First, we have merely glimpsed the glory of God—a few small drops in the ocean of His splendour. We live with a constant thirst for more of Him in our lives. Second, we live in the knowledge that we're a broken people—healed in part, yet still so fragile. We are unfinished worshippers, longing to be whole. Lastly, we exist as strangers in a foreign land—painfully aware of the troubles that surround us and the many lost hearts that have not discovered Jesus. Looking through the lens of heaven, our hearts ache to usher God's Kingdom into these situations.

Yet these three tensions do not make us worse worshippers. Instead, they sharpen our devotion, strengthening our resolve to persevere in faith. We see only in part, yet what we see is enough to give us hope and purpose on our journey. And as we go about our worship here and now, we keep one eye fixed on the horizon, confident that one day the imperfect will disappear, and we shall know fully, even as we are fully known. C. S. Lewis summed it up best: 'If I find in myself a desire which no experience in this world can satisfy, the most probable explanation is that I was made for another world.'[6]

10
the unending worshipper

When I stand in glory
I will see His face,
And there I'll serve my King forever
In that holy place.[1]

Here and now, we don't see clearly. As *The Message* puts it, we're 'squinting in a fog, peering through a mist' (1 Corinthians 13:12). But one day we shall see God face-to-face.

We'll be completely *unveiled* worshippers, seeing in full what we see only in part now. We will become the perfect *unquenchable* worshippers, for there'll be nothing to quench our devotion. No more tears, no more troubles, no more pain. We will be the ultimate *undignified* worshippers, no doubt joining the twenty-four elders as they throw themselves before the heavenly throne. That day will bring a freedom in praise the likes of which this world has never seen. Every distraction to our worship will have passed away. No more temptations, and no more enticements. Completely *undivided* worshippers, we will stand in the very presence of God, and He alone will consume every heart.

I recently came across what must be Charles Wesley's most bizarre hymn. It's a song about death. The first two lines came as a bit of a shock:

> Ah, lovely appearance of death!
> What sight upon earth is so fair?[2]

Had he finally lost it? So desperate to write thousands of hymns that he started coming up with any old nonsense? On first hearing, it sounds more like a horror film script than a song you'd sing in church. But delving deeper, we soon realise he might not be quite so far off the mark as we thought:

> How blest is our brother, bereft
> Of all that could burden his mind!
> How easy the soul that has left
> This wearisome body behind!
> Of evil incapable, thou,
> Whose relics with envy I see,
> No longer in misery now,
> No longer a sinner like me.[3]

Standing over the body of his dead friend, Wesley was reflecting on the race this man had run, and the path ahead of him now.

He would never sin again, never be troubled, never be tempted or ashamed. Wesley is pleased for him—maybe even a bit jealous.

Charles Wesley wasn't the only one to think like this. In his letter to the Philippians, the apostle Paul debated whether it would be better for him to 'stay' or 'go':

> Yet what shall I choose? I do not know! I am torn between the two: I desire to depart and be with Christ, which is better by far; but it is more necessary for you that I remain in the body. (Philippians 1:22–24)

One verse earlier, Paul declared that, for him, 'to live is Christ and to die is gain' (v. 21). We hear the 'dying would be gain' bit, but it's important also not to pass by the other part of the verse—the fact that, right here and now, 'to live is Christ.' In other words, on this earth, we can find Christ. We can worship and encounter Him. We can remain in Him, and He will remain in us. That way we don't slip into an escapist mentality, consumed only with the thought of heaven as some kind of eternal escape route. Paul knew that to die is gain; it's better by far, simply because it means more of Christ. But *this* life is not just a dress rehearsal or a waste of time. We can live with Jesus and for Jesus, ushering in His Kingdom right here and now.

We'd do well to get in line with Paul's outlook on life. We're a people who know where we're headed. We are on a journey with a breathtaking destination. We are running a race with an incredible prize. The inheritance which lies ahead will be altogether glorious.

And though we won't see in full until then, let's not forget that we can at least know in part now. C. S. Lewis helped to explain it:

> Meanwhile of course we are merely … tuning our instruments. The tuning up of the orchestra can be itself delightful, but only to those who can, in some measure, however little, anticipate the symphony.[4]

For now, we only experience the tuning up of our instruments. It's a curious, formless noise, and yet strangely charming, because we hear something of our eternal destiny resounding in it. We hear echoes of the perfectly inspired symphony we shall one day be a part of. But for now, the tuning up has a surprising beauty all of its own.

To end this book, I'd like to return to Charles Wesley; a man who, from the day he was saved, tuned his heart to the Lord, and spent fifty years writing 6,500 songs of praise. At the age of eighty-one, feeble and on his deathbed, he composed one final hymn. Too frail even to write, he dictated these six short lines to his wife:

> In age and feebleness extreme,
> Who shall a helpless worm redeem?
> Jesus, my only hope Thou art,
> Strength of my failing flesh and heart.
> O could I catch one smile from thee,
> And drop into eternity![5]

Here was a man who'd spent his life on Jesus. It's evident even from this one hymn that he knew the friendship of the Lord. For

Wesley, to live was Christ. And yet, because he knew where he was going—or, more specifically, to whom he was going—to die would be gain. 'O, could I catch one smile from thee, and drop into eternity!' The last words of an unsatisfied worshipper. The first words of an unending worshipper.

An eternity with Jesus in our sights, we are all unending worshippers. Let us run with determination the race marked out for us (Hebrews 12:1). Straining towards what lies ahead, let's press on to win the prize for which God has called us heavenward in Christ Jesus (Philippians 3:13–14).

Amen.

'Grace to all who love our Lord Jesus Christ with an *undying* love' (Ephesians 6:24).

notes

preface

1. Augustine, 'Sermon 34,' *The Works of Saint Augustine: A Translation for the 21st Century,* Park III-Sermons, vol. 11: Sermons 20–50, trans. Edmund Hill, ed. John E. Rotelle (Brooklyn, NY: New City Press, 1990), 168.

1: the unquenchable worshipper

1. Fanny Crosby, quoted in S. Trevena Jackson, *This Is My Story, This Is My Song* (Belfast: Emerald House, 1997).
2. Ibid.
3. Eugene Peterson, *The Message of David* (Basingstoke, UK: Marshall Pickering, 1997).
4. Bernard W. Anderson, *Out of the Depths* (Louisville, KY: Westminster John Knox Press, 2000), 3.
5. Ibid., 60.

2: the undone worshipper

1. Richard J. Foster and Emilie Griffin, eds., *Spiritual Classics* (New York: Renovaré, 2000), 224.
2. François Fenelon, *Talking with God* (Brewster, MA: Paraclete Press, 2009), 64.

3: the undignified worshipper

1. Oswald Chambers, *The Golden Book of Oswald Chambers: My Utmost for His Highest* (New York: Dodd, Mead & Co., 1935), 73.
2. William Barclay, *The Mind of Jesus* (New York: HarperCollins, 1976), 199.
3. Fred Pratt Green, 'When in Our Music God Is Glorified' © 1972 Hope Publishing Company.

4: the unpredictable worshipper

1. William Barclay, *The Mind of Jesus* (New York: HarperCollins, 1976), 197.
2. Gary A. Furr and Milburn Price, *The Dialogue of Worship* (Macon, GA: Smyth and Helwys Publishing, 1998).
3. Gene Edwards, *The Divine Romance* (Carol Stream, IL: Tyndale, 1993).
4. Michael Jackson, 'You Are Not Alone,' *HIStory* © 1995 Epic.
5. Cardinal Suenens, quoted by David Watson, *Called and Committed* (Wheaton, IL: Harold Shaw, 2000), 75.
6. C. S. Lewis, *Letters to Malcolm* (Orlando, FL: Harcourt, 2002), 5.
7. Oswald Chambers, *The Golden Book of Oswald Chambers: My Utmost for His Highest* (New York: Dodd, Mead & Co., 1935), 126.

5: the unveiled worshipper

1. William Barclay, *The Revelation of John,* vol. 1 (Louisville, KY: Westminster John Knox Press, 2004), 58.
2. Anthony Bloom, *Beginning to Pray* (Mahwah, NJ: Paulist Press, 1970), 12.
3. William Barclay, *New Testament Words* (Louisville, KY: Westminster John Knox Press, 1999), 56.

6: the unstoppable worshipper

1. Thomas Jackson, *The Life of the Rev. Charles Wesley* (London: John Mason, 1841), 373–74.
2. Dietrich Bonhoeffer, *The Cost of Discipleship* (New York: Touchstone Books, 1995), 89.
3. Dietrich Bonhoeffer, Geffrey B. Kelly, F. Burton Nelson, *A Testament to Freedom* (New York: HarperCollins, 1995), 495.

4. Beth Nimmo and Darrell Scott, *Rachel's Tears* (Nashville: Thomas Nelson, 2000), 91–92.

5. Smith Wigglesworth, *The Anointing of the Spirit* (Ventura, CA: Regal, 1994), 161.

6. William Barclay, *The Mind of Jesus* (New York: HarperCollins, 1976), 216.

7: the unnoticed worshipper

1. François Fenelon, *Talking with God* (Brewster, MA: Paraclete Press, 2009), 17.

8: the undivided worshipper

1. William Barclay, *The Mind of Jesus* (New York: HarperCollins, 1976), 189.

2. Ibid., 190

3. Charles Wesley, 'Crucified with Christ,' 1740. Public domain.

4. William Cowper, 'Oh, for a Closer Walk with God,' 1769. Public domain.

5. Richard Foster, *Celebration of Discipline* (New York: HarperCollins, 1988), 161.

6. Matt Redman, 'The Heart of Worship,' *Intimacy* © 1998 Kingsway's Thankyou Music.

7. A. W. Tozer, *Whatever Happened to Worship?* (Camp Hill, PA: Christian Publications, 1985).

9: the unsatisfied worshipper

1. Matt Redman, 'Intimacy,' *Intimacy* © 1998 Kingsway's Thankyou Music.

2. Eugene Peterson, *A Long Obedience in the Same Direction* (Downers Grove, IL: InterVarsity Press, 2000), 56.

3. Matt Redman, 'The Father's Song,' *The Father's Song* © 2000 Kingsway's Thankyou Music.

4. Jürgen Moltmann, *Theology of Hope* (Minneapolis: Fortress Press, 1993), 21.

5. I'm indebted to Bishop Graham Cray for much of the teaching in this section.

6. C. S. Lewis, *Mere Christianity* (New York: HarperCollins, 2001), 137.

10: the unending worshipper

1. Keith Green, 'There is a Redeemer,' *Songs for the Shepherd* © 1984 Ears to Hear Music/Birdwing Music/BMG Songs Inc./EMI Christian Music Publishing adm. by Copycare, PO Box 77, Hailsham BN27 3EF.

2. Charles Wesley, 'On the Corpse of a Believer,' 1746. Public domain.
3. Ibid.
4. C. S. Lewis, *Reflections on the Psalms* (Orlando, FL: Harcourt, 1986), 97.
5. Robert Morgan, *Near to the Heart of God* (Grand Rapids: Revell, 2010), 97.

BE BOLD BRIGHT BRILLIANT
LIVING BOLDLY AND SHINING BRIGHTLY FOR THE GLORY OF GOD
MIRROR BALL
MATT REDMAN
IN MIRROR BALL,
Matt Redman reminds us that even when we feel insufficient to reflect God's glory, God can shine through us as a light radiates through a prism. Living in this truth will transform how we view our words, our relationships, our daily lives.
YOU AND YOUR WORLD WILL NEVER BE THE SAME.
800.323.7543 • DavidCCook.com
David C Cook
transforming lives together